UFOs

BY SHARON DALGLEISH

WWW.APEXEDITIONS.COM

Copyright © 2022 by Apex Editions, Mendota Heights, MN 55120. All rights reserved. No part of this book may be reproduced or utilized in any form or by any means without written permission from the publisher.

Apex is distributed by North Star Editions:
sales@northstareditions.com | 888-417-0195

Produced for Apex by Red Line Editorial.

Photographs ©: iStockphoto, cover (UFOs), 1 (UFOs), 10–11, 12–13, 15, 19, 29; Unsplash, cover (background), 1 (background); Shutterstock Images, 4–5, 6–7, 8–9, 14, 18, 22–23, 24–25, 26, 27; Universal History Archive/Universal Images Group/Getty Images, 16–17; World History Archive/Alamy, 21

Library of Congress Control Number: 2021915681

ISBN
978-1-63738-166-3 (hardcover)
978-1-63738-202-8 (paperback)
978-1-63738-271-4 (ebook pdf)
978-1-63738-238-7 (hosted ebook)

Printed in the United States of America
Mankato, MN
012022

NOTE TO PARENTS AND EDUCATORS

Apex books are designed to build literacy skills in striving readers. Exciting, high-interest content attracts and holds readers' attention. The text is carefully leveled to allow students to achieve success quickly. Additional features, such as bolded glossary words for difficult terms, help build comprehension.

TABLE OF CONTENTS

CHAPTER 1
A STRANGE SIGHT 5

CHAPTER 2
OUT OF THIS WORLD 11

CHAPTER 3
SPREADING STORIES 17

CHAPTER 4
TRUE OR FALSE? 23

Comprehension Questions • 28
Glossary • 30
To Learn More • 31
About the Author • 31
Index • 32

CHAPTER 1
A STRANGE SIGHT

A fisherman is alone at sea. Suddenly, a round object hovers above his boat. It's smooth and shiny. He has no idea what it is.

Some legends tell of alien spaceships visiting Earth.

The air beneath the strange shape hums. The boat's engine stops. Next, tons of fish swirl to the surface. They churn the water around the boat.

In some stories, UFOs send out beams of light. They can lift or move objects.

UFO stands for "unidentified flying object."

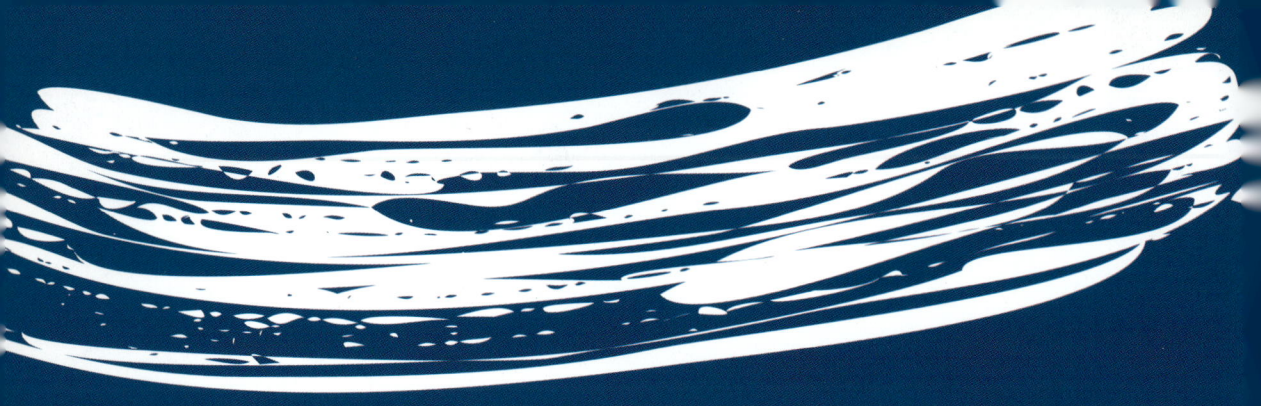

The fisherman runs below deck to get his camera. When he returns, the strange object is gone. So are the fish. Everything is back to normal.

ODD EFFECTS

People describe weird things happening near UFOs. Cars stop or won't start. TVs blink. Radios stop working. In some stories, the UFOs land. They leave behind tracks or burns.

CHAPTER 2
OUT OF THIS WORLD

Many UFOs look like flying discs or bright lights. Some dart or move quickly. Others hover in one place.

Some UFOs float above the ground. Others seem to follow cars, airplanes, or boats.

People usually see UFOs in **remote** places. Many are spotted in deserts. Others appear over lakes or oceans.

Hundreds of UFOs have been seen in deserts in North and South America.

One story said UFOs flew like saucers skipping across water. So, people began calling them "flying saucers."

Some people believe that UFOs are spaceships. They say **aliens** fly them. In some stories, aliens **abduct** people or animals. The aliens study or talk to them.

What aliens look like depends on the story. But people often say aliens are bald and have big eyes.

Some aliens attack or steal things. Others just want to interact with people.

THE CE SCALE

The CE scale describes different types of UFO **sightings**. CE1 means just seeing UFOs. CE2 is finding their tracks or effects. CE3 means aliens are present. Higher numbers describe ways of **interacting** with aliens.

Disk Craze

CHAPTER 3
SPREADING STORIES

People have seen strange objects in the sky for many years. But interest in UFOs really took off in the 1940s. In 1947, a pilot saw nine glowing objects. He said they flew very fast.

In the 1940s, many newspapers reported on UFO sightings.

That same year, a rancher in New Mexico found metal **wreckage** in a field. News stories said it was part of a spaceship that crashed.

Many UFO fans travel to New Mexico. They visit museums and locations related to famous UFO sightings.

Area 51 is in Nevada. The road to reach it is called Extraterrestrial Highway.

AREA 51

Area 51 is a testing site for the US military. Its work has been kept secret for many years. Some people say it studies aliens. Others say crashed UFOs are kept there.

In 1961, a couple claimed aliens abducted them. Their story became very famous. Many similar stories began to appear.

In some stories, aliens erase people's memories.

Betty and Barney Hill said a UFO chased their car and then took them inside.

CHAPTER 4
TRUE OR FALSE?

Many UFOs are **optical illusions**. For example, one UFO turned out to be lights reflected against the sky.

Clouds and weather sometimes create lights or shapes that look like spaceships.

Other objects may get mistaken for UFOs. Some **supposed** UFOs are actually planets or comets. Others are birds or balloons flying through the air.

The planet Venus shines brightly in the night sky. It's sometimes mistaken for a UFO.

People who study UFOs are called ufologists.

Some UFO stories are made up. People make fake photos or **evidence**. They try to trick others. However, some UFOs remain a mystery.

Some videos or photos of UFOs are illusions.

Stories tell of UFOs lifting people or animals into the air.

JUST A HOAX

In 1897, a farmer said a UFO abducted one of his cows. Many newspapers printed his story. Later, people learned it was a **hoax**. A woman overheard him bragging about making it up.

COMPREHENSION QUESTIONS

Write your answers on a separate piece of paper.

1. Write a sentence that explains the main idea of Chapter 2.

2. Would you like to see a UFO? Why or why not?

3. When did interest in UFOs begin to take off?
   - **A.** in 1897
   - **B.** in the 1940s
   - **C.** in 1961

4. Which event would be a CE3 on the CE scale?
   - **A.** A person sees a UFO in the sky.
   - **B.** A person sees aliens land and walk out of a UFO.
   - **C.** A person sees tracks in a field that seem to be made by a UFO.

5. What does **churn** mean in this book?

*Next, tons of fish swirl to the surface. They **churn** the water around the boat.*

    A. to make ice cream
    B. to mix or stir
    C. to stay very calm

6. What does **spotted** mean in this book?

*People usually see UFOs in remote places. Many are **spotted** in deserts.*

    A. seen by people
    B. eaten by animals
    C. covered in small dots

Answer key on page 32.

GLOSSARY

abduct
To kidnap or carry off.

aliens
Creatures that come from planets other than Earth.

evidence
Information that tells what happened or if something is true.

hoax
A trick to make someone believe something that is not true.

interacting
Talking with someone or doing something with them.

optical illusions
Things that trick people's eyes, so what they think they see is different from what is really there.

remote
Far away from where most people live.

sightings
Times and places when something is seen.

supposed
Guessed or claimed but not known for sure.

wreckage
Material from something that has crashed or is broken.

TO LEARN MORE

BOOKS

Abdo, Kenny. *Area 51*. Minneapolis: Abdo Publishing, 2020.

Oachs, Emily Rose. *UFOs*. Minneapolis: Bellwether Media, 2019.

Tyler, Madeline. *UFO Investigators*. New York: Gareth Stevens Publishing, 2019.

ONLINE RESOURCES

Visit **www.apexeditions.com** to find links and resources related to this title.

ABOUT THE AUTHOR

Sharon Dalgleish lives in Sydney, Australia. She enjoys watching the moon rise over the beach. She has never seen a UFO, but she will keep looking!

INDEX

A
abducted, 14, 20, 27
aliens, 14–15, 19–20
Area 51, 19

C
CE scale, 15
comets, 24

D
deserts, 12

F
fake, 26
flying saucers, 13

H
hoax, 27
hovering, 5, 11

L
lakes, 12
landing, 8
lights, 11, 23

N
New Mexico, 18

O
oceans, 12
optical illusions, 23

P
planets, 24

S
spaceships, 14, 18

T
tracks, 8, 15

Answer Key:
1. Answers will vary; **2.** Answers will vary; **3.** B; **4.** B; **5.** B; **6.** A

INDEX

A
ancient cities, 21, 25, 27
Arabian Sea, 21
Atlantic Ocean, 11
Atlas, 13

D
Dwaraka, 21

E
earthquakes, 24

G
gods, 6–8, 12–14

I
India, 21, 25
islands, 5, 7–8, 11, 20, 23–24

J
Japan, 27

K
kingdom, 5, 11–12, 14

L
lost cities, 20–21

P
Plato, 17, 26
Poseidon, 7, 12–13

S
sinking, 8–9, 14, 21

T
Thera, 23–24
tsunamis, 24–25

V
volcano, 23

Answer Key:
1. Answers will vary; **2.** Answers will vary; **3.** B; **4.** C; **5.** A; **6.** C

TO LEARN MORE

BOOKS

Abdo, Kenny. *Lost Lands*. Minneapolis: Abdo Publishing, 2020.

Polinsky, Paige V. *Atlantis*. Minneapolis: Bellwether Media, 2020.

Vale, Jenna, and Ann Lewis. *Tracking Atlantis*. New York: Rosen Publishing, 2019.

ONLINE RESOURCES

Visit **www.apexeditions.com** to find links and resources related to this title.

ABOUT THE AUTHOR

Meg Gaertner is a children's book editor and writer. She lives in Minneapolis, where she enjoys swing dancing and spending time outside.

GLOSSARY

cultures
Groups of people and the ways they live, including their beliefs and laws.

currents
Streams of water or air that move in a clear direction.

erupted
Sent hot gases, ash, and lava into the air.

legend
A famous story, often based on facts but not always completely true.

moats
Deep ditches, often filled with water, that surround a place to protect it from attack.

myths
Well-known stories from the past that often include magic.

philosopher
A person who studies ideas about knowledge, reality, and right and wrong.

tsunamis
Huge ocean waves caused by underwater earthquakes or volcanic eruptions.

utopia
An imaginary place where everything is perfect.

5. What does **fertile** mean in this book?

*The land is **fertile**. Many crops grow there.*

- **A.** able to produce many plants
- **B.** shaped like a square
- **C.** filled with water

6. What does **greed** mean in this book?

*The people have gold and riches. But they want more and more. Their **greed** angers the gods.*

- **A.** a kind way to ask a question
- **B.** a new plan for ruling a city
- **C.** a strong desire for more money

Answer key on page 32.

COMPREHENSION QUESTIONS

Write your answers on a separate piece of paper.

1. Write a sentence describing the main ideas of Chapter 4.

2. Do you think Atlantis was a real place? Why or why not?

3. When did Plato write about Atlantis?

> **A.** in 9600 BCE
> **B.** in the 300s BCE
> **C.** in the 1400s CE

4. Why do some people think Thera is the reason for the Atlantis legend?

> **A.** Like Atlantis, Thera was in Japan.
> **B.** Like Atlantis, Thera was not a real place.
> **C.** Like Atlantis, Thera was destroyed suddenly.

Divers study underwater ruins to learn about the past.

A SUNKEN CITY?

Near Japan, an area of underwater rock seems to be cut into steps. Some people say ocean **currents** formed the steps. Others say the steps are from an ancient city.

However, many scientists think Atlantis is just a legend. Plato likely made up the story. He often wrote about how groups of people should behave. The story of Atlantis helped show his ideas.

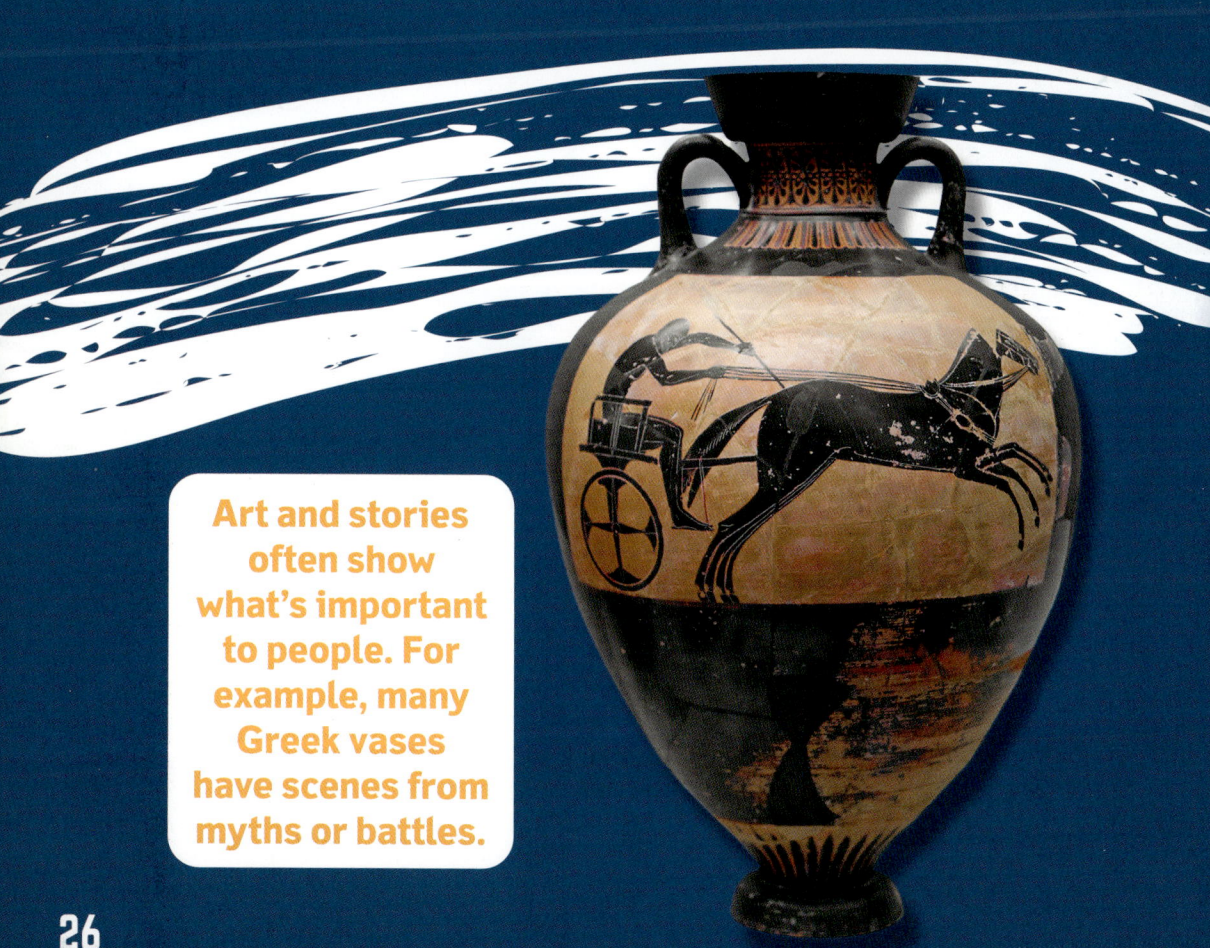

Art and stories often show what's important to people. For example, many Greek vases have scenes from myths or battles.

In 2004, a tsunami hit India. Its waves moved sand. They uncovered ruins from an ancient city.

25

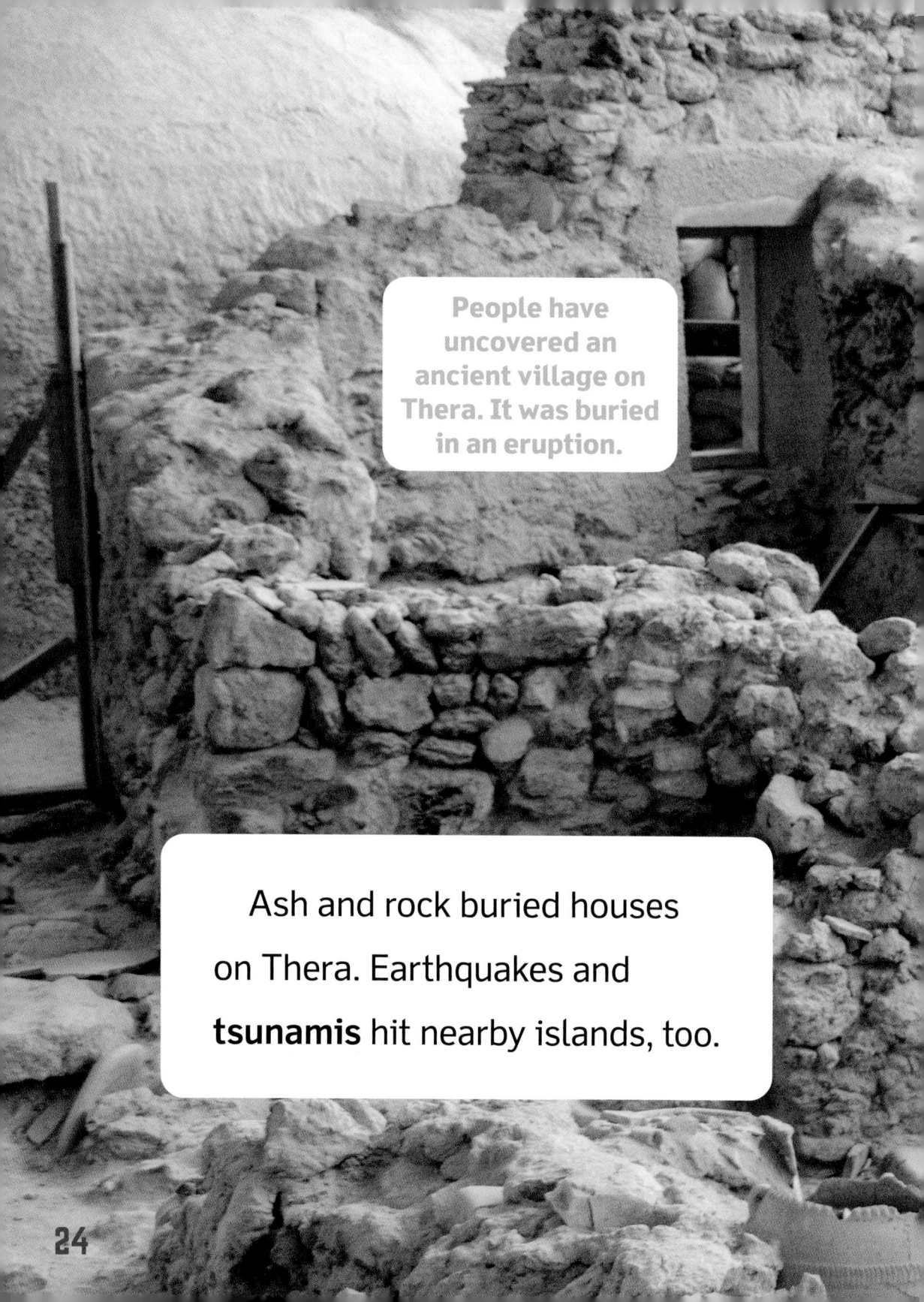

People have uncovered an ancient village on Thera. It was buried in an eruption.

Ash and rock buried houses on Thera. Earthquakes and **tsunamis** hit nearby islands, too.

CHAPTER 4
EXPLAINING THE LEGEND

Atlantis could be based on real places or events. One is the island of Thera. A volcano **erupted** there around 1600 BCE.

Thera is a Greek island in the Aegean Sea.

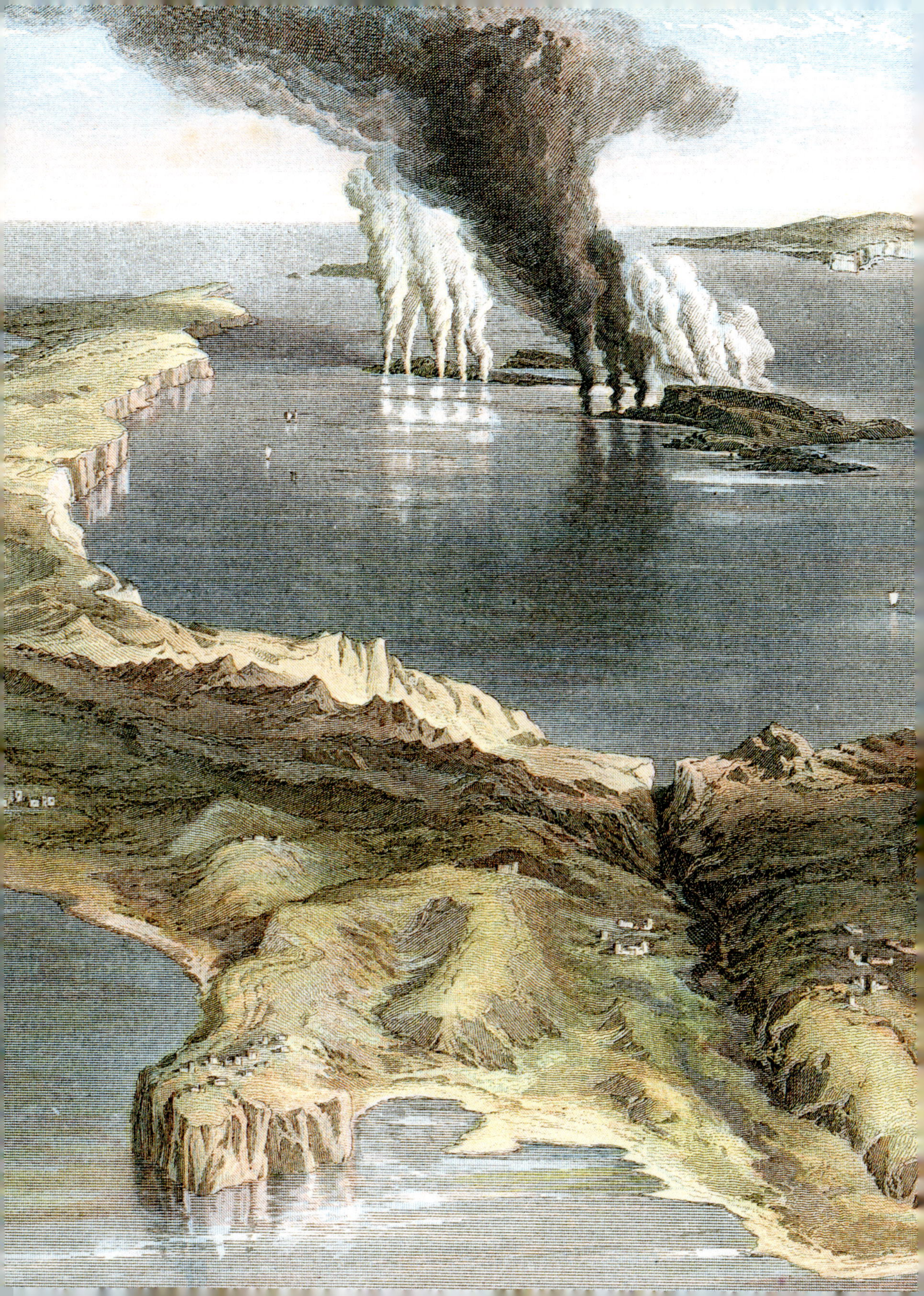

People sometimes find the remains of ancient cities buried underwater.

LOST CITIES

Many **cultures** have tales of lost cities. A text from ancient India describes the city of Dwaraka. It says the city sank beneath the Arabian Sea. People found this city in 1963.

The **legend** of Atlantis also inspired writers. They wrote their own stories about lost cities or island nations.

In some stories, people or mermaids still live in the underwater city of Atlantis.

European explorers made long trips by boat. Some told stories about what they found.

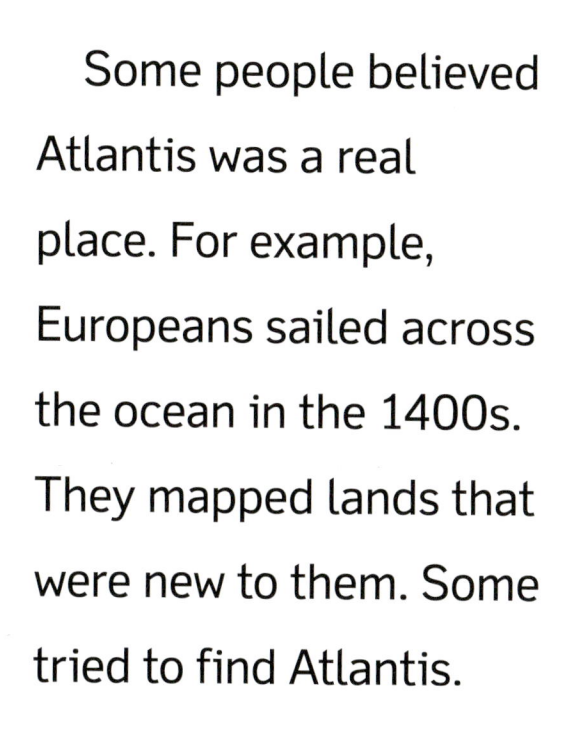

Some people believed Atlantis was a real place. For example, Europeans sailed across the ocean in the 1400s. They mapped lands that were new to them. Some tried to find Atlantis.

One scientist claimed that Sweden was Atlantis.

CHAPTER 3

THE LEGEND'S HISTORY

Atlantis first appears in Plato's writings. Plato was a Greek **philosopher**. He wrote in the 300s BCE. He said Atlantis was even older.

Plato (center left) said Atlantis existed thousands of years before his time.

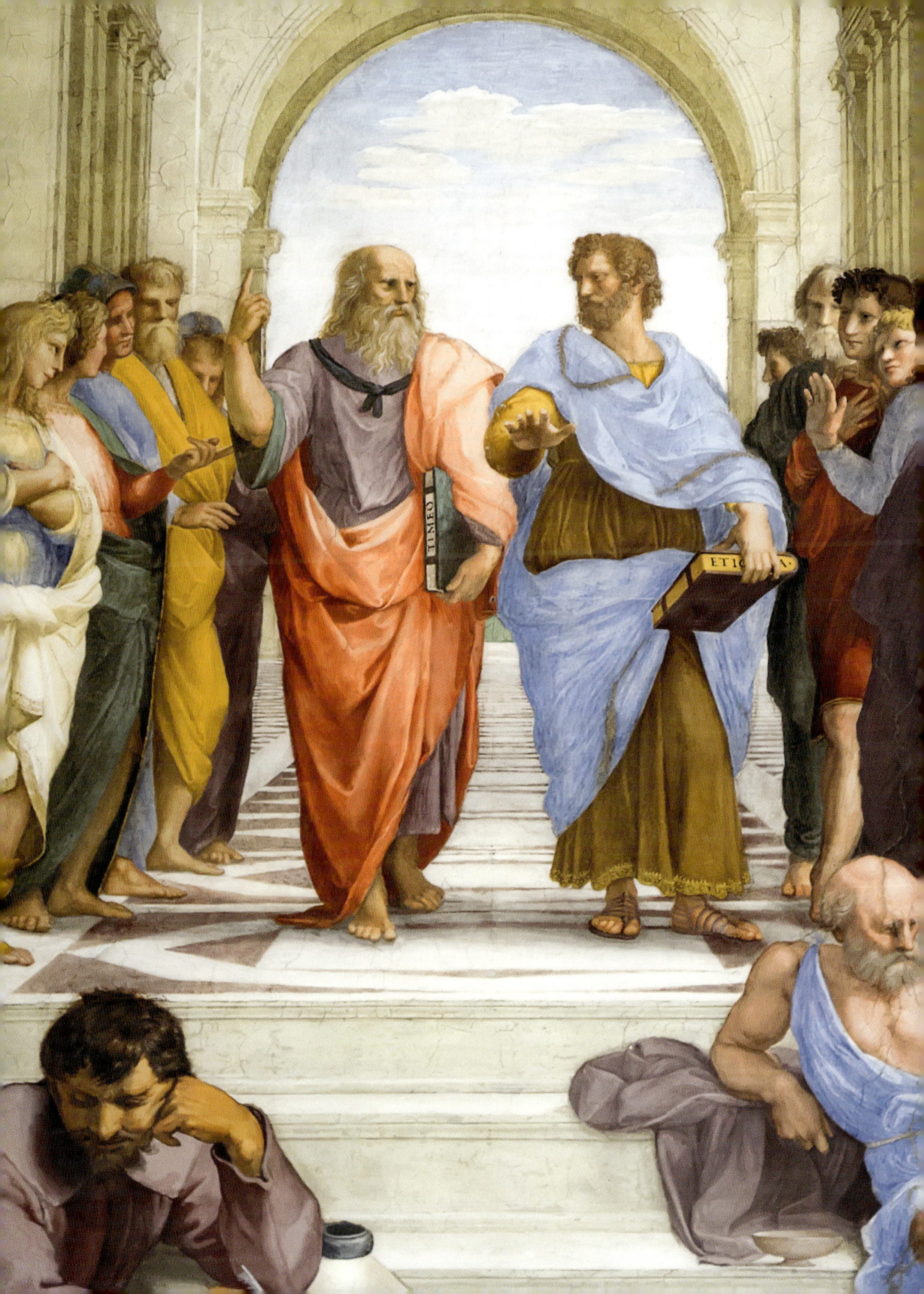
TIMEO

Some people believe parts of Atlantis are still standing somewhere under the ocean.

Stories say Atlantis disappeared around 9600 BCE.

Later, the people became greedy. So, the gods punished them. The gods made their kingdom fall. It sank into the ocean in a single day.

Poseidon's son Atlas was the city's first king.

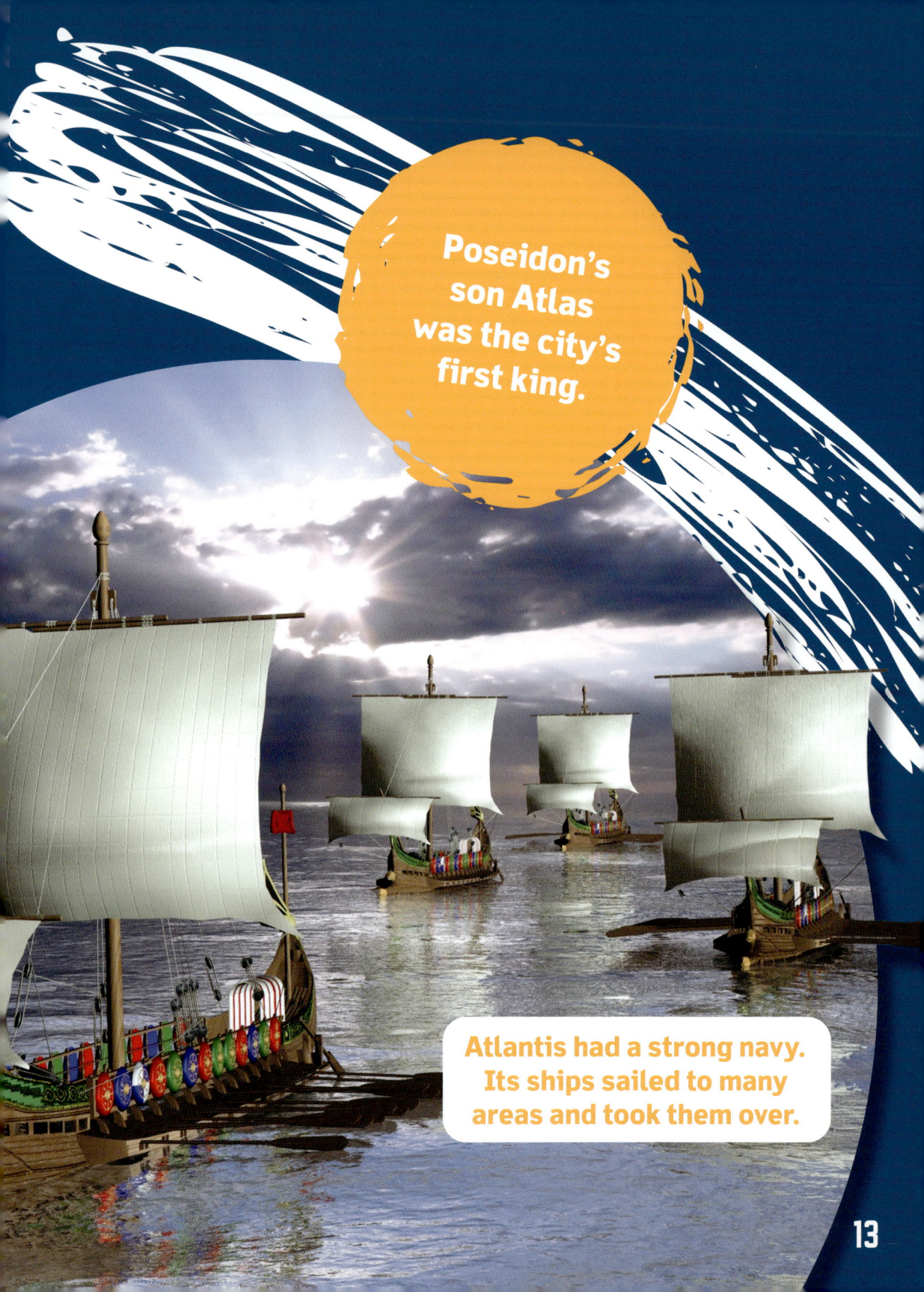

Atlantis had a strong navy. Its ships sailed to many areas and took them over.

At first, Atlantis was a **utopia**. Its people were brave and good. They were great sailors. As a result, their kingdom grew and grew.

DIVINE ORIGINS

The people of Atlantis were half human and half god. Poseidon married a human woman. They had 10 children together. Their sons became the city's rulers.

CHAPTER 2
ISLAND UTOPIA

Atlantis was an island kingdom. Stories usually say it was in the Atlantic Ocean.

Some stories say Atlantis was in the Mediterranean Sea.

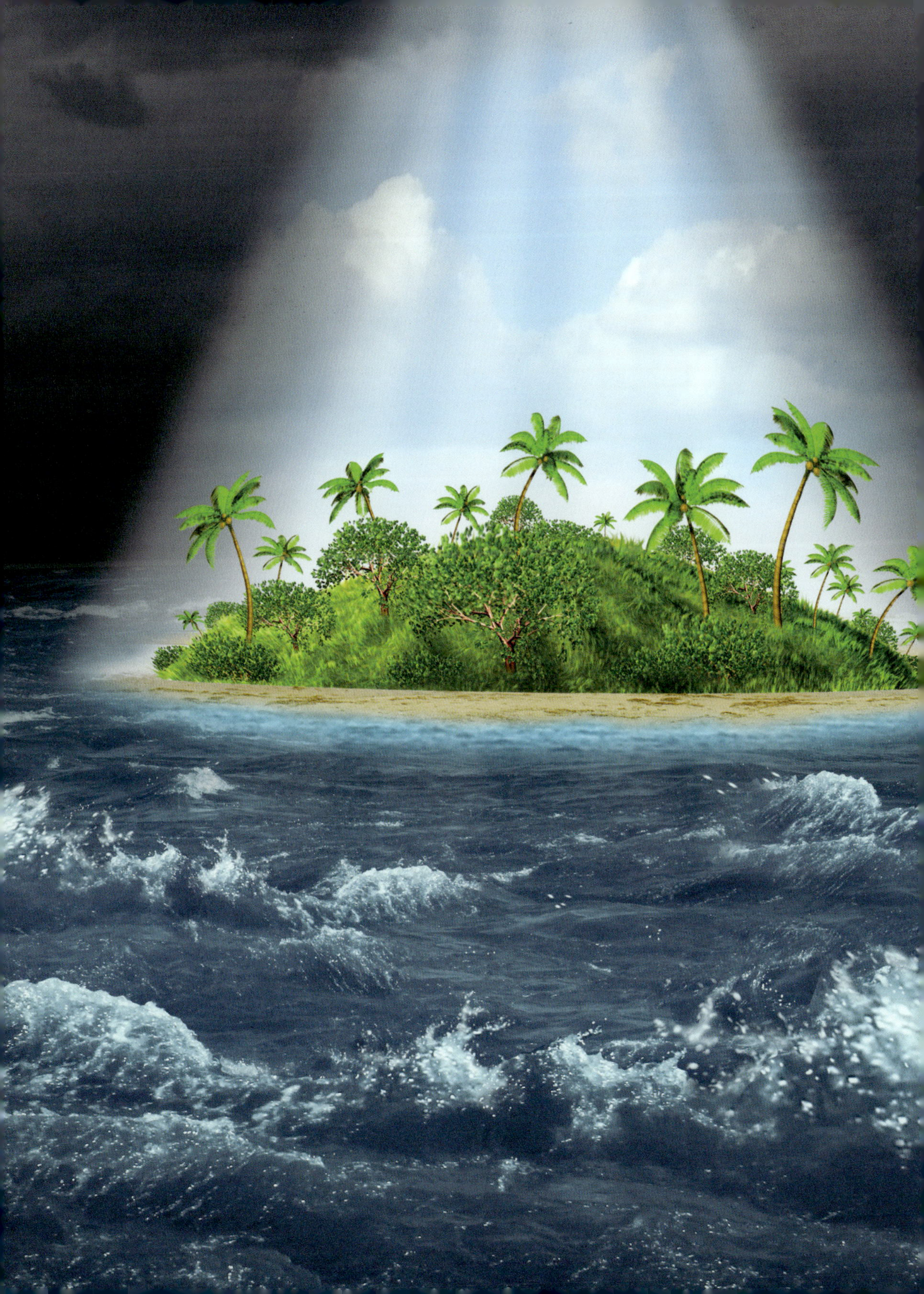

Huge waves turned the city of Atlantis into underwater ruins.

Some stories say Atlantis left a big pile of mud when it sank.

The gods make the ground shake. They make the waters rise. The island disappears beneath the sea.

Poseidon was the Greek god of the sea.

POSEIDON'S ISLAND

Greek **myths** say gods ruled different parts of Earth. The god Poseidon lived in Atlantis. He also gave the island its shape. He broke the land into rings. **Moats** formed between them.

The land is fertile. Many crops grow there. The people have gold and riches. But they want more and more. Their greed angers the gods.

Many golden statues decorated Atlantis. Some of its buildings had gold walls.

CHAPTER 1
A LOST KINGDOM

A kingdom spreads across a large island. One main city sits in the center. Rings of land and sea surround it. Together, they form the island of Atlantis.

Bridges crossed the waterways on the island of Atlantis. They led to the main city.

TABLE OF CONTENTS

CHAPTER 1
A LOST KINGDOM 5

CHAPTER 2
ISLAND UTOPIA 11

CHAPTER 3
THE LEGEND'S HISTORY 17

CHAPTER 4
EXPLAINING THE LEGEND 23

Comprehension Questions • 28
Glossary • 30
To Learn More • 31
About the Author • 31
Index • 32

WWW.APEXEDITIONS.COM

Copyright © 2022 by Apex Editions, Mendota Heights, MN 55120. All rights reserved. No part of this book may be reproduced or utilized in any form or by any means without written permission from the publisher.

Apex is distributed by North Star Editions:
sales@northstareditions.com | 888-417-0195

Produced for Apex by Red Line Editorial.

Photographs ©: Shutterstock Images, cover (foreground), cover (background), 1 (foreground), 1 (background), 4–5, 6, 7, 8–9, 10–11, 12–13, 14–15, 16–17, 20, 21, 24–25, 26, 27, 29; iStockphoto, 18–19, 22–23

Library of Congress Control Number: 2021915682

ISBN
978-1-63738-159-5 (hardcover)
978-1-63738-195-3 (paperback)
978-1-63738-264-6 (ebook pdf)
978-1-63738-231-8 (hosted ebook)

Printed in the United States of America
Mankato, MN
012022

NOTE TO PARENTS AND EDUCATORS

Apex books are designed to build literacy skills in striving readers. Exciting, high-interest content attracts and holds readers' attention. The text is carefully leveled to allow students to achieve success quickly. Additional features, such as bolded glossary words for difficult terms, help build comprehension.

ATLANTIS

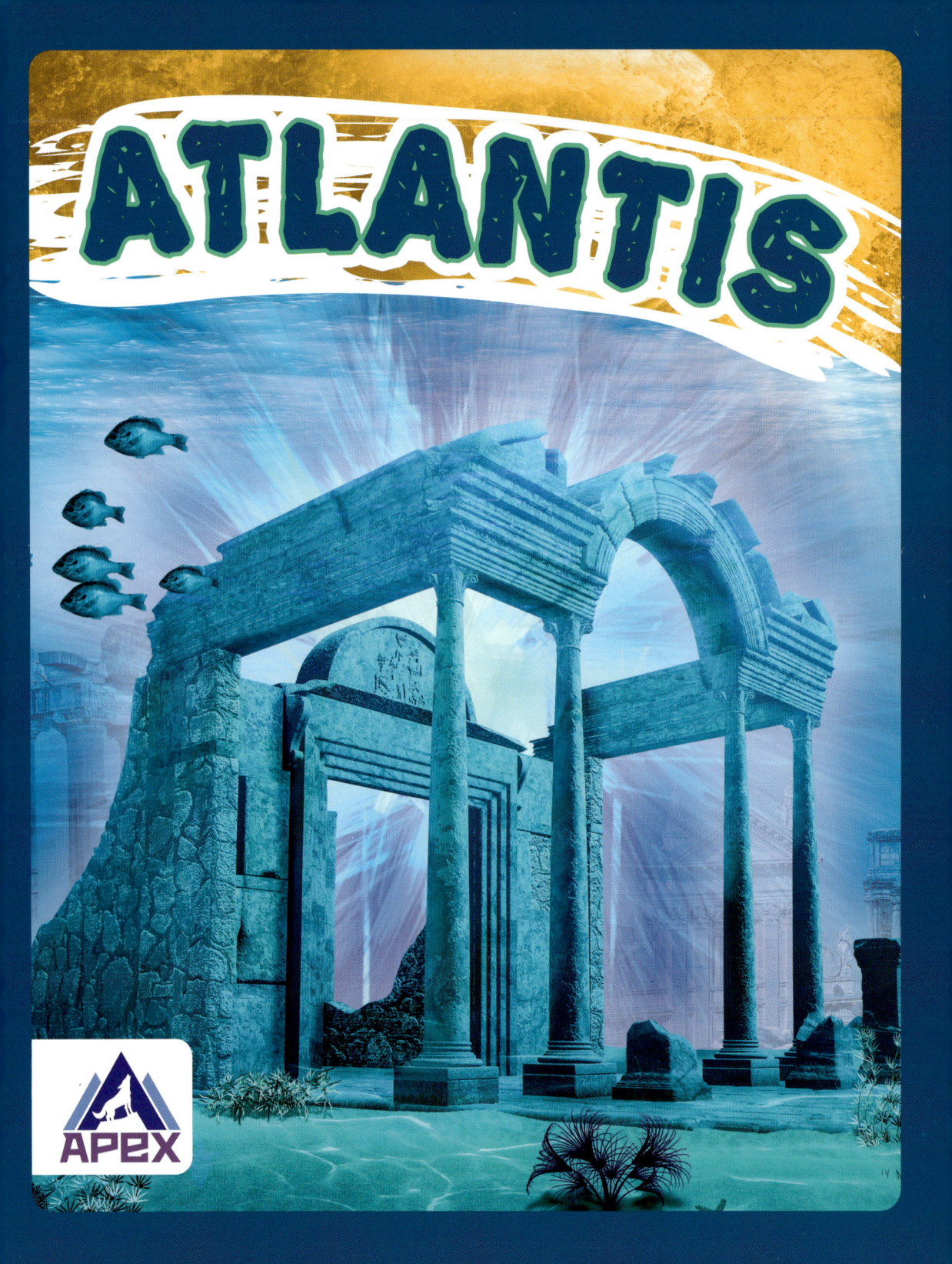

BY MEG GAERTNER